FORGED IN LOVE

~Utkarsh Prakash~

CONTENT OF THE BOOK

1.A Love She Never Understood

→ Describe author's feelings, how he fell, and how she judged his love not because she disliked him, but because she didn't believe in love itself.

2.My Fifth Confession, My Worst Breakdown

→ Talk about the recent confession, the emotional chaos, how it affected author's mental health and studies—especially the maths exam.

3.Losing the Happiest Version of Me

→ Before her, author was joyful and full of life. After the rejections, especially this last one, he began losing that version.

4.Why Did I Love So Truly?

→ Reflect on the innocence of author's love, the questions he ask himself now, and the emotional scars left behind.

5.Functioning Without Her: A Daily Battle

→ How hard it is to focus on life, studies, and dreams. Even surviving the day becomes tough.

6.Still Holding On: 0.1% Hope

→ Despite knowing the truth, he still believe in miracles—how that tiny hope gives him a reason to keep breathing.

7.Cursed for Loving?

→ The spiritual pain, how he questions God, and wonder if he is being punished for loving too purely.

8.This Is Not Just Love, It Was My Life

→ Realization that for you, she wasn't just a crush—she was the center of Author's existence.

9. Why Her Only? Why Not Someone Else?

→ This chapter is author's raw answer to the question everyone keeps asking. It's not about her being perfect—it's about how his *soul recognized hers*. He saw flaws, pain, distance, but still, his heart chose her and never changed its mind.

Chapter 10: The Final Truth — I Chose Her, Forever

→ Even if he never get her love in return, he have already chosen her—for life. He planned not just a relationship, but a *home*, a *life*, a *forever*. He didn't just fall in love— He *committed his entire existence* to her. And even now, that commitment stands unshaken.

Acknowledgement

Writing *Forged in Love* was never just about telling a story—it was about surviving one. It's the voice of a boy who loved deeply, lost silently, and lived every day carrying a heart that still beats for someone who never understood.

To **AA**, even though you never loved me back, you unknowingly became the reason I kept breathing, kept believing. You will never know the storms you helped me survive or the dreams I built with you in mind. This book is my truth, and you will forever be a part of it.

To those who are reading me for the first time—I invite you to explore the roots of this story in my first book, ***I Still Love You***. It captures the raw emotions, my silent battles, and how one-sided love shaped the boy behind these pages. If you wish to understand where this journey began, start there.

To my friends and family who saw the tears I never spoke of, thank you. And to every reader who has ever loved truly, painfully, and purely—this book is for you.

And finally, to the broken yet brave version of myself—this is your story, your courage, your heart on paper.

With all my soul,
Utkarsh Prakash

Chapter 1: A Love She Never Understood

They say love is supposed to be mutual, that it's supposed to grow between two hearts. But what if only one heart beats with belief, while the other has given up before the story could even begin? That's where my love lived. In a space between hope and silence. In the gap between everything I gave, and everything she didn't understand.

I didn't fall for her the way stories tell you love happens. There was no sudden moment. It was gradual—like sunrise. First, a spark of interest, then a soft warmth, and eventually, a light so blinding that it filled my entire world. I didn't choose her. My heart did. My soul did. It wasn't about beauty or perfection. It was about something I couldn't explain—something deeper, unshakable. I saw her and knew that something within me had shifted forever.

She never asked for my love. I never forced it on her. But in every silent glance, every little gesture, I gave her pieces of myself. I loved her in silence when words were too heavy, and I loved her in hope when rejection was a constant answer. I wasn't foolish—I knew she wasn't in love with me. But still, I believed. Because what I felt wasn't desire. It was destiny.

The truth is—she didn't reject me because she hated me. That thought never crossed my mind. I know her heart wasn't made of stone. I believe she just didn't believe in the kind of love I offered. Maybe life broke her faith in love long before I came into the picture. Maybe she had learned that love equals pain, and she decided never to believe in it again. And maybe, just maybe, I reminded her of something she was trying hard to forget.

But that didn't stop me from loving her with everything I had.

People often asked me, "Why are you doing this to yourself? Why love someone who clearly doesn't feel the same?" I never had an answer. How do you explain to someone that love is not something you choose to feel—it's something that chooses you? I didn't wake up one day and decide to make her my world. It happened slowly, then all at once. And when it did, I couldn't imagine a world where she wasn't the center.

But what broke me wasn't her rejection. It was the way she judged my love—as if it was just a teenage crush, just another passing emotion. She didn't see the depth, the truth, the purity of it. She thought I was immature. She thought I didn't understand love. But the irony is—what I felt for her was the most real thing I've ever known.

And that's the pain I carry. Not that she didn't love me back, but that she never saw how true my love was.

She thought I was loving an illusion. But I was loving her reality—the way she smiled, the way her eyes sparkled when she talked about something she loved, the way she walked past me in the corridor without knowing that every step echoed in my heart for hours. She didn't know that her existence was the reason I got out of bed some mornings. That even a glance from her was enough to keep me going through the worst days.

She judged me because she didn't understand me. Not because she was cruel, but because she didn't believe someone could actually love like that.

And maybe I can't blame her. In today's world, love is often confused with attraction, and connection with lust. Maybe she thought I was just another boy lost in a fantasy. But I wasn't. I wasn't dreaming. I was feeling. Truly. Deeply. Completely.

She never read the letters I never wrote. She never heard the screams I kept inside. She never saw the way I smiled through the pain, just because she was near. And maybe she never will. That's the reality I have to accept.

But this love—it wasn't for her to validate. It was mine to carry.

And in carrying it, I changed. I broke. I rebuilt. I cried. I smiled. I died inside. And still—I loved.

This love forged me. Not into someone stronger. But into someone *real*. Someone who knows what it means to give without receiving, to believe without proof, to stay when everything inside you is screaming to walk away.

She never understood. And maybe she never will.

But this love—this fire—it burned through me, and even though I lost myself in it, I wouldn't undo a single flame.

Because no matter what I lost, I know one thing:

I was **Forged in Love**.

The fire of love that I entered didn't just burn—it melted me, reshaped me, and left me standing in the ruins of what I used to be. I never thought that giving my all would leave me feeling so empty. Yet here I am, still whispering her name in prayers, still hoping she finds happiness—even if it's not with me.

You see, I didn't just fall in love with a girl. I gave my soul to someone who couldn't see its value. Not because she was blind, but because the world had taught her not to trust light anymore. I wasn't her enemy, but I became the reflection of what she feared—love that stayed, that didn't demand, that only gave.

My love wasn't perfect, but it was pure. I didn't love her for what she could give me. I loved her because she existed, and to me, that was enough.

Maybe this chapter isn't about her not understanding me. Maybe it's about me learning that not every soul is ready for the kind of love that scars and heals at the same time. That some hearts have built walls so high that even the softest love can't climb over.

But even if she never understands, I will never regret loving her.

Because in this burning, in this breaking—I found something eternal.

I found that even in losing her, I discovered myself.

And that, too, is love.

She once told me, with a casual laugh, that it was all just "timepass." She didn't mean to hurt me, I suppose, but those words hit me like a thousand knives. How could she not see the depth of my love? How could she not understand that this wasn't just a fleeting feeling or a momentary distraction? I wasn't looking for a passing affair or something that could be brushed off. I was looking for a forever, a bond that would stand the test of time. But to her, it was just another "phase," just something that would eventually fade away.

I remember the way she said it, as if she was gently letting me down, without realizing how much she was tearing me apart. It wasn't the words that hurt the most, but the meaning behind them. To her, my love was nothing more than a temporary distraction, something to pass the time. She didn't see it for what it was—something real, something pure, something unshakable.

After that, everything began to fall apart.

The breakup, though inevitable, hit me harder than anything I had ever experienced. I thought I could handle it.

After all, I had prepared myself for the worst. But nothing could have prepared me for the emptiness that followed. It was as if the ground beneath me had vanished, leaving me to fall endlessly into nothingness.

And the worst part? The isolation. The way people started looking at me. I didn't just lose her—I lost myself in the process. The rejection, the heartbreak, the feelings of inadequacy—all of it began to seep into my mind. I became a shadow of who I once was. I couldn't focus on my studies, my friends, or anything that once brought me joy. The depression set in, and I felt like I was suffocating. Every morning was a struggle, every night a torment.

What hurt even more was the judgment. The way people started to look at me differently. I began to notice whispers when I passed by, the sideways glances, the silent conversations that paused when I entered the room. It was as if my worth had been tied to her, and once that connection was broken, I was nothing. I could almost hear the murmurs: *"He's that guy who loved too much." "He's the one who couldn't get over her."* And worse, *"He's the one who made a fool of himself."*

In a world that values strength and independence, loving someone so deeply seemed like a weakness. It made me feel small. I began to wonder—did loving someone so much really lower your reputation? Was it so shameful to care for someone, to feel something so pure, even if it was unreturned?

I found myself questioning everything—my worth, my actions, and my place in the world. The world around me seemed so harsh, so unforgiving. People didn't care about the love you gave—they only cared about how you looked from the outside. And when that love was unreciprocated, you were just another story of failure.

Did loving her, truly and deeply, make me weak? Did it make me foolish? Did it make me less of a person?

I don't have an answer to that. But what I know now is that my love for her wasn't a weakness. It was a testament to the kind of person I am—a person who believes in love, who dares to love even when the world tells him not to. Yes, it hurt. Yes, it tore me apart. But it also made me who I am today. And if loving her made me weaker in the eyes of others, then let that be their judgment. I wouldn't trade my love for her, not for anything in this world.

I loved her, and even if she never understood that love, it didn't diminish its value.

In the end, the heartbreak and depression that followed her rejection became my reality. But even in that pain, I found strength. The love I gave her may have been misunderstood, but it was mine to hold—

mine to cherish, no matter how much it hurt.

We never came into a relationship. No sweet moments shared, no promises made. There was no 'us'—only me. Only me, loving her in silence, with no response, no acknowledgment. And yet, I kept believing, kept hoping that maybe one day, she would understand.

But that was the problem, wasn't it? She never understood.

I remember the first time she told me that my feelings were just "timepass"—a passing phase. The words stung like nothing I had ever felt before. How could she say that? How could she dismiss everything I felt as something so trivial, so insignificant?

It wasn't "timepass" to me. It was everything. Every moment, every thought, every breath I took felt connected to her. She was the first thing on my mind in the morning and the last at night. I had no idea how to turn it off, how to stop the love that was bursting out of me.

But she didn't see it that way.

She judged me. Not because she didn't like me, but because she didn't believe in the kind of love I had for her. Maybe she had been hurt before, maybe life had taught her that love wasn't something to trust, that it was fleeting and shallow. Or maybe she simply couldn't understand how a person could love so deeply without expecting anything in return.

And that hurt more than I ever imagined it could. It wasn't just her rejection—it was the way she dismissed me. Like I wasn't worthy of such deep emotions. Like my feelings didn't matter. That judgment cut through me in ways words couldn't fully explain.

It was easy for her to write me off, to dismiss me as just another boy with a fleeting crush. But for me, this wasn't a crush—it was a storm inside my heart, a fire that I couldn't extinguish no matter how much I wanted to.

After that, I tried to move on. I tried to let go of my feelings for her, but the more I tried, the more I realized how much of my world had revolved around her. I couldn't function properly without her in my thoughts. Every time I saw her, every time I caught a glimpse of her smile or heard her laugh, the hope would flare up again, even though I knew I was just fooling myself.

And then came the breakup—not because we were together, but because she had already made up her mind that I wasn't someone she could accept. I never even had the chance to show her the depth of my feelings. She had already decided who I was, and what I was capable of. And she didn't believe that I could love her the way I did.

The heartbreak, the confusion, the rejection—it all came crashing down on me in waves. But that wasn't even the hardest part. The hardest part was dealing with the judgment from everyone around me. People looked at me differently. They saw my unrequited love as a weakness. They thought I was foolish, that I was wasting my time.

I felt it—the whispers, the side glances, the judgment that hung in the air like a dark cloud. Loving someone who didn't love you back didn't make you stronger or braver. It made you vulnerable, open to ridicule, and it felt like everyone could see the cracks in my armor.

But I didn't care about their judgment—not at first. What hurt the most was the feeling of being misunderstood. It wasn't just that she didn't love me back; it was that she never understood what I was offering. It wasn't something temporary or shallow. It was real. It was raw. It was pure.

But she couldn't see that. And no matter how much I tried to explain, no matter how many times I tried to make her understand the depth of my feelings, it was never enough.

And that's when I realized something—love, true love, isn't always about being accepted. It's not always about getting the other person to see your worth or understand your feelings. Sometimes, love is about giving everything you have, even if it's never returned. Even if it's never understood.

I could've walked away. I could've stopped caring, stopped loving. But I didn't. I couldn't. Because in some strange way, loving her was the only thing that made sense in this chaotic world. Even if it meant enduring the pain, even if it meant losing my reputation and my peace of mind, I couldn't stop loving her.

But that didn't mean it was easy. The rejection, the judgment—it was a weight I carried every single day. People didn't understand why I still loved someone who didn't love me back. They didn't see the depth, the purity of it. And in a world where love was often reduced to fleeting moments or physical attraction, my feelings for her felt out of place.

But in the end, I realized that I didn't need anyone else to validate my love. I didn't need her to love me back. What mattered was that I loved truly, honestly, and deeply. And that was enough.

It wasn't easy. It wasn't simple. But it was real.

And even though she never understood, even though she judged me and rejected me, I would never regret loving her. Because in the end, loving her had forged me into someone who could love with everything, even if it meant losing it all.

Chapter 2: My Fifth Confession, My Worst Breakdown

It was May 10th, 2025. Exactly one year since I first saw her. Exactly one year since my heart was ignited with something so deep, so pure, that it burned with an intensity I couldn't control. The fire of love, the kind that makes you believe in impossible things, in dreams, in a future that feels like it's meant to be. And here I was again, standing on the precipice of hope, about to confess for the fifth time.

One year of silent love. One year of longing and pain. One year of giving without receiving. And yet, here I was, still holding onto that 0.1% of hope that perhaps, just perhaps, she would see me differently this time. Maybe this time, she would accept me. Maybe this time, she would understand.

I had confessed to her four times before. Four times, each one with its own set of emotions—hope, vulnerability, and finally, devastation. The first time was the hardest. The second time, I thought it might be easier, but it wasn't. The third time, I convinced myself it was just a part of the process. And the fourth time, I was numb. But today, on May 10th, 2025, I was standing before her again. But this time, I was prepared for anything. Or so I thought.

It had been a year of silent admiration, of watching her from a distance, and each time I saw her, my heart still skipped a beat. Nothing had changed. I still loved her with the same intensity. I still carried her in my thoughts, in my soul. But nothing was different on her side. I knew that. But that tiny hope still flickered inside me like a candle in a storm.

I approached her, my heart pounding in my chest, and the words I had rehearsed for days flowed out of me. I told her that I loved her—again. I told her that my feelings had only grown stronger with time. I told her that I couldn't stop loving her, no matter how much time had passed.

And for the first time, she didn't say no immediately.

Her silence was the worst part. It was like she was processing it, trying to figure out how to respond, whether she could say something different this time. But then, the words came, and when they did, they shattered everything I had built inside myself.

"I can't accept," she said. "Because all these are just timepass and nothing. After a breakup, it hurts a lot, and your reputation also goes down. I can only be your friend and nothing more than that. If you don't agree, then don't talk to me."

Her words echoed in my head. "Timepass." "Nothing." "Reputation." Those words felt like a punch in the gut. I could feel my chest tighten, my throat close up, and all I wanted to do was scream. I had never imagined it would be like this. I had never imagined that after all this time, after everything I had poured into her in silence, she would reduce my love to nothing but a passing phase.

Her words were poison, dripping with the weight of rejection. They weren't just a rejection of my love—they were a rejection of everything I was. A rejection of my sincerity, my honesty, my pain. She didn't see the depth of my feelings. She didn't understand how much I had given. And to her, it was just "timepass."

I wanted to argue. I wanted to scream at her, to tell her that she didn't understand, that what I was feeling was real. But in that moment, I couldn't speak. My words felt useless, empty, like they had no meaning.

How could someone think so little of something so pure? How could she see the love I had for her as just a game, just something that didn't matter in the grand scheme of things? I had given her my heart, and she had thrown it away like it was nothing.

And then she said it—those final words: "If you don't agree, then don't talk to me."

It was like she was sealing the door shut. There was no room for me anymore. No room for hope. No room for love. And the worst part? She made it seem like the only option was to accept her friendship or lose even that.

In that moment, something inside me broke. It was like I was standing at the edge of a cliff, and all the hope I had held onto for so long was swept away in an instant. I couldn't breathe. I couldn't think. The pain was overwhelming. My body went numb, and all I could hear was the deafening sound of my own heart breaking.

I turned away from her, not because I wanted to, but because I didn't know what else to do. My heart was bleeding, and my mind was spiraling out of control. The world around me felt like it was collapsing. I wanted to die. I wanted to end it all right there, because the pain of her words, the pain of her rejection, was too much to bear.

For the next two days, I was lost in a haze of depression. I didn't eat, I didn't sleep. I couldn't focus on anything. The weight of her words crushed me, and I found myself wishing for a way out. I couldn't escape the thoughts that kept swirling in my head. "Timepass." "Nothing." "Reputation." Those words haunted me, playing over and over again like a broken record.

And the worst part? I couldn't even cry. It was like my emotions had shut down completely. I felt hollow. Empty. Like a shell of the person I used to be.

It wasn't just the rejection that hurt—it was the way she had judged me. The way she had made me feel like I was beneath her, like my love wasn't worth anything. It was like I was invisible to her, like everything I had ever felt, every moment I had spent loving her, didn't matter at all.

But that wasn't even the hardest part. The hardest part was that I still loved her. Despite everything. Despite her rejection. Despite her words. I still loved her. And I didn't know how to stop.

I remember that night, lying in bed, staring at the ceiling, praying to God. I wasn't asking for anything. I was just begging for the pain to stop. I wanted to disappear. I wanted to forget about everything—the love, the rejection, the hope, the despair. I wanted it all to go away.

But the pain didn't go away. It stayed with me, gnawing at my insides. And that's when I realized something—something that hurt almost as much as her words: the love I had for her would never fade. It would never go away, no matter how much I wished it would.

I had loved her with everything I had. And in the end, it didn't matter. I wasn't good enough. I wasn't the one. And she would never see me the way I saw her.

But no matter how much it hurt, I couldn't stop loving her. Even if it meant losing myself, even if it meant losing everything I had, I couldn't stop loving her. Because that's what love is. It's not something you choose. It chooses you. And no matter how much it hurt, I couldn't let go.

The days after that confession felt like an eternity. Every moment was a battle. Every thought, every breath, was consumed by the weight of her words. The rejection wasn't just about her not loving me back. It was about the way she had dismissed everything I had felt, the way she had reduced my love to something insignificant. And that hurt in ways I couldn't even explain.

That night, I lay in bed, staring at the ceiling, my mind a blur of painful thoughts. The tears wouldn't stop. They came in waves, crashing over me, leaving me gasping for air. I wasn't crying because of her rejection alone. I was crying because of the hopelessness that had settled inside me. The hopelessness that had been slowly growing for the past year, but now it felt like a part of me that I couldn't escape.

I cursed myself over and over. I cursed the very day I was born. I cursed this world, this time—this Kalyug. The world where love seemed to mean nothing, where everything was about fleeting moments, shallow connections, and broken hearts. And yet, I had loved so deeply, so purely. I had given her everything, and it still wasn't enough. It was never going to be enough.

I began to question everything. Why was I born in this time? Why was I born into a world that didn't value love the way I did? Why was I born into a place where people didn't understand the depth of emotion, the purity of feelings that I had to offer?

Was it a curse? Was I destined to suffer? Because that's what it felt like. Like a cruel joke. I kept thinking, maybe God had a plan for me. But what kind of plan was this? Was this what I was meant to experience? To love someone so deeply, only to have them tear me apart, to watch them turn away from everything I had given them?

It felt like a punishment.

I wondered—did God know all along? Did He know that she could never be mine? Did He send her into my life knowing that I would fall for her, knowing that it would destroy me in the end? Was this the test I had to endure, to teach me something about myself, about love? Or was it just His cruel joke, sending me someone I would never have, only to watch me suffer day after day?

I cursed Him. I cursed the very idea of love. I cursed the universe for making me believe in something that was so painfully out of reach. I cursed my own heart for making me feel emotions I couldn't control. I wondered why I couldn't just shut it all off. Why couldn't I just stop loving her? Why did it hurt so much to be in love with someone who would never love me back?

I thought of all the prayers I had sent out, all the wishes I had whispered into the night. I had begged for a chance to be with her. I had prayed for her to understand, for her to see me, for her to love me back. But none of it had been answered. All my prayers had gone unnoticed. God didn't hear me. Or maybe He did, but He just didn't care. Maybe He was laughing at me from above, watching me slowly break apart under the weight of my own feelings.

I wondered if He had ever really loved anyone. I wondered if He knew what it felt like to love someone with every fiber of your being and still have them turn away. To give everything you had and watch it slip through your fingers like sand.

I remember screaming at the heavens that night. It wasn't a cry for help. It wasn't a plea for mercy. It was just pure rage—rage at God, at the world, at myself.

"Why did you send her into my life?" I shouted, tears blurring my vision. "Why did you make me fall for her when you knew she would never be mine? Why did you make me weak? Why did you give me a love so strong, so pure, only to make me watch it burn in the end?"

I wanted to die that night. I wanted to escape this pain, this never-ending ache in my chest. I wanted to leave this world, this cruel Kalyug, and never come back. I couldn't stand it anymore. The hopelessness. The loneliness. The pain. The empty feeling that consumed me every single day.

And all I could think of was her. Her face, her smile, the way she walked into my life like a dream, only to shatter it into a million pieces.

She was the reason I had fallen apart. She was the reason I had lost myself. But she would never know. She would never understand the depth of my pain. She would never know the extent to which her rejection had destroyed me.

And I hated myself for loving her. I hated myself for caring so much. I hated myself for giving her the power to break me.

But I couldn't stop. I couldn't stop loving her. No matter how much I cursed God, no matter how much I wished I could erase the love I had for her, it wouldn't go away. It was a fire that burned inside me, and even though it was consuming me, I couldn't extinguish it.

I spent the next few days in a haze of pain and self-loathing. I didn't want to face the world. I didn't want to go to school, talk to anyone, or even look at myself in the mirror. I felt like a ghost, like I wasn't even alive anymore. I had no purpose. I had no reason to exist.

The days blurred into each other. I walked through life like I was underwater, disconnected from everything around me. My thoughts were consumed by her, by what she had said, by what I had lost. I couldn't focus on anything else. Everything seemed meaningless without her.

But the worst part was the feeling of emptiness. The feeling that I had lost something so important, so precious, and I would never get it back. It wasn't just her rejection that hurt—it was the loss of myself. It was the realization that in loving her, I had given up parts of myself. And now, I didn't know who I was anymore.

It felt like I was losing everything. My happiness. My peace. My identity.

And the worst part? I didn't know how to get it back.

In the days that followed her rejection, something changed inside me—something that made me feel like I was spiraling further away from myself. It was as if, overnight, I became a different person.

One moment, I was lost in a love so pure that I couldn't imagine my life without it. The next, I was consumed by hatred for myself, even though my love for her hadn't changed.

I woke up the next morning, and everything felt different. The world seemed colder, more distant. The colors outside my window seemed muted, as if the life had been drained out of everything I once held dear. I had never felt so empty, so hollow.

But what was worse was the anger that burned inside me. The anger that wasn't directed at her—no, I could never hate her—but at myself. I was angry at myself for being weak, for being foolish enough to believe that she could ever feel the same way. I was angry for giving my heart to someone who would never understand me. I was angry for being the fool who thought love could conquer everything, when all it did was leave me broken.

I started to hate myself for how much I had allowed myself to be vulnerable. For how much I had loved someone who would never love me back. I hated how weak I had become in her presence, how much I had allowed myself to fall. The very things that once made me proud of my love for her—its purity, its selflessness, its depth—now felt like a curse.

How could I have been so blind? How could I have loved someone who couldn't even see the value of what I was offering? I asked myself these questions over and over again, each time feeling more disgusted with myself. I wanted to erase all the feelings I had for her. I wanted to forget how much I had cared, how much I had sacrificed. I wanted to pretend I had never loved her at all.

But no matter how much I hated myself, no matter how much I wished I could shut off my heart, my love for her never changed. It remained as it was, unshaken and unwavering, even as my self-loathing grew.

It was like a war within me—my love for her was like a fire that kept burning, while my hatred for myself was like an ocean trying to drown it. But no matter how much I tried to bury it, my love refused to be extinguished. It lingered, silent and steadfast, a constant ache in my chest.

I wished I could have stopped loving her. I wished I could have walked away, as easily as she had, and freed myself from the pain.

But the truth was, I couldn't. My love for her wasn't something I had control over. It wasn't a switch I could turn off. It was a part of me, a part of my soul, and no matter how much I hated myself for it, it was never going to disappear.

And that was the most painful part— knowing that despite all the hurt, despite all the rejection, I still loved her. I still wanted her to understand. I still wanted her to see the truth in my heart.

But I couldn't change what had happened. I couldn't change the way she had judged me, the way she had dismissed my love. And I couldn't change the way I had fallen so deeply for her, knowing that she would never love me the same way.

So, I was left with this twisted contradiction: a love that remained the same, despite everything, and a self-hatred that grew each day.

And in that conflict, I felt like I was slowly disappearing. The more I hated myself, the more I lost myself. The more I questioned my worth, the more I doubted everything I had believed in. I no longer knew who I was, who I had become. All I knew was that I was drowning in a sea of confusion, pain, and regret.

I had become my own enemy. The one person who should have been there for me, the one person who should have loved me unconditionally—was myself. But instead, I stood in front of the mirror every day and saw nothing but a failure.

But despite all of it, my love for her remained. Unfathomable. Unyielding.

And that was the only truth left in my life.

Chapter 3: Losing the Happiest Version of Me

Before her, I was a different person. I used to be the one who laughed the loudest, smiled the brightest, and carried a carefree spirit that made every moment feel light. I was the friend who always found joy in the little things, the one who could crack a joke even in the toughest of times. I lived without fear, without worry—my heart was full of hope and optimism. Life was a celebration, and I was the one leading the dance.

I didn't have a care in the world back then. The future was just a blur of possibilities, each one more exciting than the last. I didn't overthink, I didn't second-guess myself. I woke up every day with a smile, ready to take on whatever came my way. My life was full of laughter, and I had no idea how precious that version of myself was until it began to slip away.

Then came her.

I didn't expect it. I didn't ask for it. But somehow, without even realizing it, I gave her everything. Every laugh, every smile, every carefree moment—I gave it all to her, hoping that one day, she would understand. But that's not what happened. What I didn't see coming was the way my love for her would transform me, piece by piece, into someone unrecognizable.

At first, it was just a small change. I started thinking about her more than I should have. My heart, once free and light, began to feel heavy with expectation, with hope. Then came the rejections—each one chipping away at the person I used to be. Each time she didn't accept me, each time she judged my love as insignificant, a part of me died inside. I no longer found joy in the things that used to make me laugh. The world felt a little duller, and I couldn't seem to shake the weight of what I was carrying.

The worst part wasn't the rejection—it was how I changed. I started to overthink everything. Every word she said, every action she took, every moment spent near her—it all became a riddle I had to solve. I found myself questioning every little thing I did, wondering if she noticed, wondering if I was doing enough, wondering if she was even thinking about me.

I became obsessed with her. But not in a way that was healthy. My thoughts weren't just about her. They were about what I could do to win her over, to make her see me, to make her understand the depth of what I felt for her. My mind was consumed by her, and it began to take its toll on me. The joy I once had—gone. The smile I used to wear—vanished. I was no longer the carefree person I once was. I had become someone who was constantly on edge, always fearful of losing her, always doubting my own worth.

And that fear—oh, that fear—became the center of my world. The fear of losing her. The fear that she would never understand. The fear that no matter how much I loved her, it wouldn't be enough. Those fears consumed me. And with each passing day, they grew stronger, drowning out the person I used to be.

Her rejection, especially the last one, was the final blow. It confirmed everything I had feared—everything I had tried so hard to avoid. She didn't just reject my love, she rejected me, the version of me that had loved so purely, so deeply. She didn't understand that loving her had changed me. She didn't understand how much of myself I had poured into her, hoping that one day, she would see it for what it truly was.

And when she told me, "I can only be your friend," it felt like everything I was, everything I had been, crumbled into dust. The joyful, carefree person I once was was gone. In his place was someone who could only think about her—about the love that would never be returned, about the life I had lost.

I no longer recognized myself. I was a shadow of who I used to be, consumed by overthinking, by fear, by tears that never seemed to stop. I had given everything to someone who didn't even see me. And now, I was left with nothing but emptiness.

All I wanted was for her to understand. All I wanted was for her to see that what I offered wasn't just a passing moment, but a love that could have been everything. But now, it was too late. She had already decided that my love wasn't worth it. And in that decision, I lost the happiest version of me—the version that had once smiled so freely, laughed without worry, and lived with an open heart.

Now, I was just someone who existed, waiting for something that would never come.

Before all of this, I was someone who lived with no burdens on my shoulders. I was the one people turned to for a laugh, the one who could always find a way to ease the tension in the room. I was full of life—ready to take on any challenge with a grin on my face. I didn't know what it meant to be afraid of tomorrow because, for me, each day was a new adventure. I had dreams, ambitions, and above all, a heart that was open to whatever life threw my way.

I used to be the one who never cared about the little things. A bad day at school? No problem. A disagreement with a friend? No big deal. I could always find a way to shake it off. I was strong, confident, and carefree. My life was my own, and I lived it with a passion that fueled everything I did. I was unstoppable.

But then I saw her.

She walked into my life like a storm, and in her presence, everything changed. It wasn't an instant attraction that I felt for her. It wasn't the kind of love people talk about in fairy tales. It was deeper. It was something I couldn't explain—something that grew slowly, like roots taking hold deep inside my soul.

At first, it was just a quiet admiration. Her smile, her laugh, the way she carried herself—it all caught my attention. But soon, my feelings for her began to consume me. She became the center of my universe. I started to care about things I never cared about before—like how she felt, what she thought, whether she noticed me. I was no longer the carefree, confident person I once was. I became someone who spent his nights wondering if she would ever look my way, someone who was constantly lost in thoughts about her.

The moment I realized that my feelings for her were not just passing emotions, but a love that ran deep—too deep for me to control—it was too late. I had already let myself fall. And once I fell, there was no going back.

But with each rejection, I found myself falling deeper into a place I couldn't escape. It started with the simple feeling of not being enough, of never measuring up to whatever standards she had in her mind. With every "maybe" and "we'll see" that she threw my way, I started to lose pieces of myself. I thought, *Maybe this time. Maybe I can convince her. Maybe this time she'll understand me.* But the more I tried, the more I lost the person I once was.

She never saw my love for what it truly was. She didn't see the depth of it, the purity, the fire that burned inside me. To her, it was just a passing phase—a "timepass," as she once put it. She never understood that it wasn't just a fleeting emotion for me. It wasn't just about wanting her. It was about needing her, about believing that life without her would be incomplete. She didn't understand that I wasn't asking her for something temporary. I was asking her for everything.

And that's what broke me the most. Not her rejection, but the way she dismissed my love. She didn't just say no. She made me feel like my love didn't matter. Like it was insignificant. And that hurt more than I could ever express.

The worst part wasn't just losing her, though. It was losing myself in the process. I gave her everything—my heart, my hopes, my future. I poured everything I had into loving her, and in return, I became a shell of the person I once was.

Now, I'm a stranger to the person I used to be. I don't recognize the face that stares back at me in the mirror anymore. Where once there was laughter, there is only silence. Where once there was hope, now there is only doubt. I wake up every day feeling like I'm drowning in a sea of overthinking, self-doubt, and fear. Fear of never being enough. Fear of never being seen for who I truly am. Fear of losing her, even when I know I never had her to begin with.

Every moment of joy, every ounce of happiness I once had, has been replaced by an overwhelming need to prove myself. To prove that I am worthy of her. But no matter how hard I try, I can never seem to break through the wall she's built around her heart. And that hurts. It hurts more than I can describe.

It's as if I've become a prisoner in my own mind, shackled by my love for her, trapped in a cycle of endless regret and self-pity. I can't escape it. I can't stop thinking about her, even when I know that she will never feel the same. Every thought, every breath, every heartbeat is consumed by her. And with each passing day, I feel more and more like a ghost of the person I once was.

I miss the old me. I miss the person who could laugh without a care in the world. I miss the person who could look at the future with hope and excitement. But now, all I have is fear. Fear of losing her. Fear of never being good enough. Fear of a life without her.

But still, despite everything, I can't stop loving her. No matter how much I lose myself, no matter how much it hurts, I can't stop loving her. And maybe that's the most tragic part of it all—how I gave everything to someone who never even asked for it.

Sometimes, when I'm alone in my room, staring at the ceiling in the dark, the silence screams louder than any noise ever could. That silence isn't just absence—it's her absence. And it eats me alive. I feel too much... too deeply... and yet, there's no one to feel it with. No one to share the weight I carry in my heart. No one to understand the ache that has settled in my bones.

I feel lonely—not just in the literal sense, but in the kind of way that leaves you hollow inside. The kind of loneliness where you're surrounded by people, but still feel like no one can reach the part of you that's breaking. The world moves on, but I remain stuck—stuck in the memories, the feelings, the what-ifs.

And the worst part, the most foolish mistake I made—was planning a future with her. I didn't just imagine dates or phone calls or a simple "yes" from her. I imagined a life. A life where I'd work hard, build a name, and she'd be there beside me. I saw myself achieving everything—not for pride, not for ego—but just to give her the world. I thought someday she'd see it, recognize my love, and maybe say, "Yes, you're the one."

But now, those dreams are like broken glass. Every piece cuts deeper the more I try to hold onto it. And no matter how much I bleed, I can't let them go—because they were all I ever wanted. I replay those imagined futures in my mind: walking hand-in-hand, smiling without pain, talking without fear, loving without limits. But they're not real. They never were. And knowing that shatters me more than her rejection ever did.

It hurts more than hell—not just because she didn't love me, but because I gave her my entire world in my head, and now I'm left to live in the ruins of those dreams. I built a castle with her name carved on every stone, and now I stand alone, in the ashes, with no one to even remember what it was.

She didn't just walk away from me—she walked away with the version of me that used to smile freely. And now, here I am, broken pieces held together by fading hope, crying silently at night and pretending I'm fine during the day.

I've started to hate myself—not because I did something wrong, but because I gave everything to someone who didn't even ask for it. I hate myself for loving this deeply, for caring this much, for planning a forever when she didn't even want a tomorrow with me. I hate how I let her become my everything, when I was just another page in her story—one she never even wanted to read.

But even in all this pain, one truth remains unchanged: my love for her hasn't died. And maybe, just maybe, that's what hurts the most.

Chapter 4: Why Did I Love So Truly?

There are days when I just sit silently, asking myself the same question over and over again—*Why did I love so truly?* Why did I pour all that I was into someone who never asked for it, never saw it, never accepted it? Why did my heart choose her? Why couldn't I have loved halfway like others do? Why did it have to be this deep, this raw, this consuming?

It wasn't just love—it was surrender. A surrender of my laughter, my peace, my innocence. I gave her everything without a contract, without a condition, without even the assurance that she'd look back. I loved with the kind of purity this world often ridicules. A kind of love that made people call me foolish, delusional, and naive. But I wasn't any of those things. I was just... true.

There was no backup plan. No second option. I didn't love her thinking she was perfect. I loved her because she was real to me—because she existed, and that was enough. I saw her smile once, and that smile became my world. I heard her laugh, and that sound echoed in my mind like a favourite song. I watched her walk past me a thousand times, and each time felt like the first.

I remember how just one hope from her—that *maybe* she'd accept me—lit up my entire world like Diwali lights in a dark alley. I built dreams around that tiny flame. I planted futures in the soil of her maybe. And when she crushed it all on 10th May 2025, after my fifth confession, it wasn't just rejection. It was destruction. Because I wasn't hoping anymore—I was surviving on that hope.

Her words, "It's just timepass," "Breakups hurt," "Reputation goes down"—those weren't just statements. They were daggers, dipped in disbelief, thrown straight at the soul of someone who never saw his love as a game, never thought of leaving, never feared consequences—because my love was worship. Her words didn't just reject me, they destroyed every pure emotion I carried inside.

That day, I cried like never before. Not because she didn't accept me, but because my truth, my love, my soul—everything was misunderstood. I cursed myself. I cursed my destiny. I cursed God for making me feel something so divine, only to let it rot unacknowledged. I felt abandoned. Not just by her—but by the universe. It felt like God had sent her into my life just to break me down, just to remind me how fragile the human heart can be.

And even after all that, my love for her didn't change. It remained the same—unchanged, untamed. But within one day of her rejection, I started hating myself. I hated my emotions, my attachment, my helpless heart that still beat for her. I hated how I still looked for her smile in a crowd. How I still paused when someone took her name. How even after the breakdown, my heart whispered, "Maybe one day."

I stopped smiling the way I used to. I stopped laughing without a reason. The old me—the boy who used to be full of life—slowly started fading. What took over was a version who overthought every word, every memory, every what-if. A boy who cried more than he smiled. Who cared too much and received nothing in return. Who now feared love more than loneliness.

And amidst all this pain, one thing became crystal clear: the pain I carry inside me might never find its way into words. No diary, no poem, no chapter, no cry can ever truly express the weight of this love. Because this love wasn't a story—it was a lifetime.

The emotional scars she left behind, they don't bleed—but they burn. Every time I hear a love song, every time someone says her name, every time I close my eyes and remember that last conversation—I bleed inside. And the worst part? No one sees it. No one knows it. It's just me—battling the silence she left behind.

So, why did I love so truly?

Because that's the only way I know how to love.

And maybe, just maybe, that's the curse I'll carry forever.

I sit with this question every night — *Why did I love so truly?*
Why did I give her my soul when all I received in return was silence and judgment?

It wasn't supposed to be like this.
Loving someone wasn't supposed to make me hate myself.
But here I am… lost in my own head, questioning every beat of my heart, every choice I made, every prayer I offered.

I didn't love her for a reason. I didn't love
her expecting anything.
I loved her because my heart felt safe in her
presence.
Because her name had become a rhythm in
my breath.
Because even her silence felt warmer than
the world's noise.

But now, that silence haunts me.
Now, her voice, those few words of
dismissal, echo louder than anything else.

I ask myself — was it foolish to love so
innocently?
To believe that if love is true, it will one day
be seen, felt, returned?

Everyone talks about heartbreak, but no
one talks about the aftermath —
The nights you cry so hard your chest feels
like it's going to collapse.
The mornings you wake up and feel like
your soul didn't make it through the night.
The days where laughter feels like betrayal

to your pain.
And the worst part?
You still love them.
You still *wish* they'd understand.

I tried to move on.
Tried to hate her.
Tried to curse my own heart for being so
pure, so loyal, so stupid.
But how can I hate the very thing that gave
me the most real emotion I've ever felt?

This pain I carry — it's not one I can express.
Not in words, not in tears, not even in
writing.

There's no letter long enough to capture it.
No poem deep enough to explain it.
No scream loud enough to release it.

It lives in my blood now.
In the weight behind my smiles.
In the hollowness behind my eyes.
In the silence of my prayers that remain
unanswered.

People think loving someone is brave.
But no one talks about the bravery it takes
to still breathe after being left behind.
To still look at the world and try to function
when your world has already ended.

She was never mine.
And maybe that's the saddest part.
I built dreams with someone who didn't
even know they were part of a plan.
I made her my forever when she only saw
me as a passing moment.

And yet... I don't regret it.

Because this love — as painful, scarring, and
unreciprocated as it is —
Was *mine.*
Pure. Honest. Real.

Even if she never understood it.
Even if the world mocks it.
Even if it leaves me broken for life.

I'll still know that once...
There lived a boy who loved with everything
he had.

And even though he lost, he never stopped loving.

Sometimes I wonder if maybe the problem was never the love, but the world I loved in.

A world where true feelings are mocked. Where loyalty is mistaken for obsession. Where loving someone silently, purely, becomes something shameful instead of sacred.

And maybe she was just a mirror of that world.

She once said to me — *"It's all timepass. After breakups, it hurts. Reputation goes down."*
And that shattered me.

Because in those words, everything I ever believed in was crushed.
Not because she rejected me — I could live with that.
But because she reduced my love into something temporary, something meaningless.

She never knew the nights I spent praying to
God for just one chance.
She never knew that I talked to the moon
about her.
That I used to smile at her name as if it was
poetry.
That every time I passed her in the corridor,
my heart whispered — *"Please, just notice
me once."*

But she didn't.

And now, what remains is not just pain —
It's a version of myself that doesn't know
how to be happy anymore.

I look at old photos of mine, smiling, bright,
full of dreams —
And I don't recognize that boy.

He died the day my fifth confession was met
with those words.
He died the day his hope was mistaken for
pressure.
He died the day his love was treated like a
burden.

Now I walk through life carrying a body that
feels heavier,
A soul that feels emptier,
A heart that still beats her name but bleeds
with every echo.

People say — *Time heals.*
But no one talks about the kind of wounds
that time doesn't understand.
Wounds carved not by action, but by
ignorance.
By being invisible to the one who mattered
the most.

And yet, I ask again — *Why did I love so
truly?*

Because that's who I am.

I was the boy who believed love was still
sacred.
That it wasn't about relationships or labels,
but about feelings.
About seeing someone and knowing —
They are the one.

Even when they don't feel the same.
Even when it destroys you.

I've stopped asking God for miracles.
Because maybe the biggest miracle already
happened —
I loved, selflessly.

And maybe that's enough for this lifetime.

Let the world laugh. Let them call me
foolish.
Let her think it was just "timepass."
But deep inside, I know — what I felt was
divine.

I just wish the divine had answered me
back.

And you know what hurts more than her
rejection?

It's that after all this, after giving my heart,
after staying loyal when she never even
asked me to — I ended up being the boy
whose feelings no one sees. No one
understands. No one even *cares* about.

Not at school.
Not at home.
Not even in my prayers anymore — because
even God has gone silent.

There was a time I used to be the cheerful
one — always cracking jokes, helping
others, laughing loudly in my room, teasing
my siblings, humming songs while studying.
But now?

Now I sit in silence.
Stare at walls.
Answer in short replies.
My phone is silent. My mind is loud.

And no one asks why.

At home, if I speak less — I'm scolded.
If I look sad — I'm told I have an attitude.
If I make a small mistake — I'm shouted at
like I ruined everything.

But no one sees that I'm already broken.
No one sees the tears I wipe away quietly at
night.
No one hears the cries muffled into my

pillow.
No one cares that the boy they once knew is fading.

They just see a boy not behaving "normally."

But how do I explain that *normal* left me the day she did?

How do I tell them that I'm carrying a storm inside and all I ever wanted was a little understanding, a little care, just a little... love?

She didn't care.
And now it feels like no one else does either.

Sometimes I ask myself — *Was loving her truly my biggest mistake?*

But I stop that thought midway.

Because I didn't love her for what I would get.
I loved her for what I felt.

And even if it left me ruined, I can still say —
I loved her purely. Completely. Truly.

Even if the world turned its back.
Even if I became a stranger in my own
home.
Even if I was left unseen, unheard,
misunderstood.

This pain...
Maybe it can't be explained — not through
words, not through tears.

But it exists.
It breathes inside me.
It burns quietly.

And it reminds me every day of one truth —
I loved in a way this world doesn't
understand.

And maybe never will.

Chapter 5: Functioning Without Her: A Daily Battle

People say time heals everything. That wounds fade, pain lessens, and life moves on. But they never talk about the days in between—the days when waking up feels like a war, when simply getting through the hours feels like dragging a shattered heart through a battlefield.

That's what it's been like—functioning without her.

She was never mine. Not even for a day. But her presence, her existence, her smile, her silence—it gave my life rhythm. Even though she never held my hand, she held my world together. Now that she's gone— now that she's made it clear there's no future, no hope, no place for my love—I am left trying to live a life that feels like a lie.

Each day begins with an ache in my chest. Not because I miss the way she treated me, but because I miss the person I was when I believed she might care someday. There was hope, however small. Now there's only silence.

I wake up, force myself to move, and pretend everything is fine. In school, I laugh when others laugh, nod when people speak to me, write notes when the teacher explains. But inside, it's all numbness. It's mechanical. Because every second, my mind whispers her name. Every second, I remember what I lost, even though I never really had it.

I walk through corridors where she once passed. I stare at the empty seat she once sat on. I listen to the wind hoping it'll carry her voice back to me. But it never does. And I still look. Still wait.

The hardest part isn't that she didn't love me. It's that I have to keep pretending that I don't love her anymore.

When friends ask how I'm doing, I say, "I'm fine." When family tells me to focus on my studies, I nod. But what would they know about the focus it takes just to *breathe* without breaking down?

I try to keep myself busy. Books. Assignments. Future plans. But even while studying, a memory hits me—a smile she gave someone else, a moment we accidentally locked eyes, a time she almost said yes. And suddenly, I'm not in the present anymore. I'm in that memory. Stuck. Hurt. Longing.

Every day is a battle between my past and my future. My heart still clings to the memories. My mind knows I have to move on. But how do you move on from someone who lives inside you?

The dreams I had with her still haunt me. I planned a future—imagined walking beside her, working hard not just for my goals, but for *ours*. I wanted to be someone she could be proud of. But now I'm just someone trying not to fall apart.

Sleep has become a stranger. I lie awake staring at the ceiling, wondering if she ever thinks of me. Wondering if she knows how much I loved. If she knows that each rejection didn't just break my heart—it shattered my sense of self.

I'm scared of the silence now. It reminds me of her absence. I'm scared of my thoughts— they all lead back to her. I'm scared of the future—because I don't know how to live in it without her.

And yet, I survive. Day by day. Not because I'm strong. But because there's no other choice. I survive because somewhere, deep down, I still carry that tiny flicker of hope— not that she'll come back, but that I'll come back to *myself* someday.

But right now, every day is a fight. A fight to get out of bed. A fight to smile. A fight to study. A fight to act like I'm okay.

And even though I'm still breathing, the truth is—I'm barely living.

Because functioning without her is not living. It's enduring.

And it's the hardest thing I've ever done.

Chapter 6: Still Holding On – 0.1% Hope

Even after everything—after all the rejections, all the silences, and every unreturned feeling—I still find myself holding on. Not to the dreams that once made me smile, not to the promises that were never spoken, but to a tiny flicker deep within me. A 0.1% hope. As fragile as a thread in a storm, yet somehow, it has survived. And maybe, just maybe, that fragile thread is the only thing keeping me from completely falling apart.

People say hope is dangerous. And they're not wrong. Hope can build empires within your heart only to let them crumble with a single word. It can keep you alive, but also torture you every second. That 0.1% inside me—it doesn't shout. It whispers. Quietly. Telling me, "What if?" What if one day she sees what I saw in her? What if one day, even for a fleeting second, she thinks of me the way I've thought of her for what feels like forever?

I know the truth. I've seen it. Felt it. Her words were clear. Her intentions, final. And yet, there's a part of me that still looks toward the door, hoping it might open. There's a part of me that checks my phone hoping her name lights up. There's a version of me living in some alternate reality, where we're not strangers with a past, but soulmates with a future.

It's hard to explain how I keep going. Every day is a storm. I smile, but it never reaches my heart. I laugh, but it sounds foreign even to me. I study, I walk, I talk—but all with a weight pressing down on my chest. And yet, in that weight, there's still that sliver of light.

Maybe it's foolish. Maybe it's pathetic. But it's real. That hope—so tiny, so irrational—is real. I've tried killing it. Tried telling myself that it's over. That there's nothing left. But I can't. Because she wasn't just someone I liked. She was the reason my mornings felt worth waking up for. She was the reason I dared to dream, even when life was falling apart. And when someone becomes the air you breathe, how do you just stop breathing?

Sometimes I wonder if love is a curse. If my purest emotion was actually my biggest mistake. But then I remember the way I felt whenever she smiled. How my heart beat faster just seeing her from afar. That wasn't a curse. That was magic. It still is.

I hold on not because I expect a miracle, but because letting go feels like death. It feels like erasing a part of my soul. This hope, no matter how small, is what connects me to who I was before I broke. It reminds me that there was a time I could love that deeply, believe that strongly.

And so I hold on. Not because I'm waiting.
Not because I think she'll come back. But
because that 0.1% is all I have left.

In a world that took everything from me—
my smiles, my joy, my dreams—I still have
this.

A small, trembling hope.

And until it fades on its own,

I will keep breathing.

I often wonder if my hope is just an illusion.
Is it a defense mechanism, something to
shield me from the overwhelming truth that
no matter how long I wait, no matter how
deep my feelings go, the result will always
be the same—she will never be mine?

And yet, here I am. Holding on to that
tiniest thread of hope, the faintest shimmer
of light in the vast darkness of my heart.
The hope that keeps me going, that
somehow, one day, things will be different.
It's only 0.1% of hope, but it's enough to

make me wake up every morning and face the day, even though everything inside me wants to shut down and give up.

I keep asking myself why I hold on. I know the answer. I hold on because I can't imagine a world without her in it, even if it's from a distance. The 0.1% is all I have left. It's the last shred of belief that something might change, that maybe, just maybe, life will surprise me.

But the problem is that with every passing day, that hope gets weaker. The more time goes by, the more I realize how unlikely it is that she'll ever feel the same way. The reality of it hits harder with each rejection, and still, I cling to this tiny hope like it's the last lifeline I have. Sometimes, I wonder if it's a curse. That I am doomed to love her this way, forever wishing for something that can never be.

I don't want to let go. I can't. If I let go of the hope, what will I have left? Nothing.

And if there's nothing left, then what's the point of even existing? At least with the hope, I can still pretend that maybe, just maybe, something will change. Maybe I'll get a sign, a gesture, something that tells me I haven't been wrong all this time. Maybe she'll see me the way I see her. But every day, that hope is tested, stretched thinner and thinner until it's almost invisible.

It's the strangest thing. How can one person, one thought, hold so much power over me? I have tried to move on, I've tried to get rid of the hope, to tell myself that it's over, that I need to stop waiting for something that isn't going to happen. But even then, it's as if my heart refuses to listen. Every time I think I'm done, I find myself thinking of her again. And every time I think I'm not hoping anymore, a tiny spark reignites somewhere inside me.

Sometimes, I wonder if this is what true love feels like—the pain of not being able to stop loving someone, even when you know they'll never love you back. I wish I could just forget her. I wish I could go to sleep one night and wake up with no memory of the love I have for her. It would make everything so much easier. But life doesn't work that way, does it? It doesn't let go of things that easily. It keeps reminding me, day after day, of the love I have for her, and the love she'll never give back.

The 0.1% of hope is all that's left to keep me going. It's a fragile thing, but it's what makes me get up every morning and face the world. It's the reason I keep pushing forward, even though my heart is broken and my mind is a mess. I can't explain it. I just know that without that 0.1%, I would have nothing to live for.

I've realized something, though. Even though I can never have her the way I want, even though the reality is crushing and painful, this love has taught me something. It's taught me how to feel, how to truly experience life in its deepest, most emotional form. In loving her, I've learned what it means to give everything to someone without expecting anything in return. I've learned that love isn't about getting something back—it's about feeling something that consumes you entirely, that changes you, that shapes you into someone different.

That's why I can't let go of the hope. It's not just about her anymore. It's about me. It's about the person I've become in the process of loving her. Even if she never accepts me, even if she never feels the same way, I am a different person because of this love. And that 0.1% of hope—no matter how small it is—keeps me connected to that version of myself, the one who believes in something greater than just the pain.

But still, I wonder: Will I ever find the courage to let go? Or will I keep clinging to that hope, even when it's only a whisper in the storm?

Maybe, just maybe, that 0.1% will lead me to something new—something I can't even imagine yet. Or maybe it will keep me here, stuck in the same cycle, endlessly hoping for a miracle that will never come.

Either way, that 0.1% is all I have, and for now, it's enough.

Chapter 7: Cursed for Loving?

There comes a point in pain when even tears stop falling—not because the hurt is over, but because the soul begins to bleed in silence. That's what I've been living through. Not just a heartbreak, but a spiritual collapse. A soul that once prayed with faith, now trembles with doubt. A heart that once believed in love like worship, now questions if love was ever a blessing—or a curse in disguise.

Was I **cursed for loving purely**?

I ask this question to myself every night. And worse, I ask it to the skies, to the stars, to the God I once trusted blindly. I used to fold my hands and pray for her—not to make her love me, but just to keep her happy, safe, peaceful. I begged for her well-being, even if it meant she would never be mine. I thought pure love had the power to move the universe, to melt even the coldest fates.

But all my prayers? Unheard.
All my cries? Unseen.
All my devotion? Unrewarded.

What did I do so wrong that love became my punishment?

I didn't lust after her. I didn't want her for her body. I wanted her soul. I admired her smile, her way of walking, her little habits, the spark in her eyes, the way she tied her hair. I loved her silently for months, never crossing boundaries, never asking for anything more than a place in her heart. I thought maybe, just maybe, that kind of love meant something in this world.

But maybe that's where I went wrong.
Maybe in this world, pure love is a weakness.
Maybe people don't value someone who would die for them—they chase the ones who hurt them.

There were nights I would lie down, look up at the ceiling, and whisper,
"Why, God? Why did You make me love her if You already wrote in destiny that she won't love me back?"

And then I'd curse myself for even being born in this time, in this *Kalyug*—a world where love is a trend, not a truth.
Where being real is rare, and being loyal is laughed at.

I started believing that maybe I wasn't made for love. Maybe I was made to feel love, give love—but never receive it. That's how deeply cursed I began to feel. Like I was carrying some sin from a past life, paying for it now through this unbearable pain of rejection, loneliness, and emotional abandonment.

I was the boy who believed in prayers. Who thought writing her name on every last page of his notebook, praying after every meal, whispering her name while looking at the sky—all of it would make a difference.

But God stayed silent.

And so slowly, painfully, I stopped praying.

What's the point of praying when all you get is silence in return? What's the point of having faith when all it does is break you even more?

My belief in destiny started shaking. If loving someone from the bottom of your heart can bring this much sorrow, then maybe it's not love that hurts—it's the illusion that good intentions will be rewarded.

Sometimes I think, did God just send her in my life to break me? To make me feel what it's like to live with a heart full of someone who doesn't even see me that way? To teach me how it feels to love someone who walks away while you're burning alive?

It's funny, isn't it? We're told God listens to the cries of the broken. But what if He's the one who breaks us just to see how loud we can cry?

And despite everything, I still couldn't hate her.
That's the real curse.

I hated myself for loving her.
I hated God for giving me such a heart.
But I could never hate her.

Even today, I whisper her name with the same softness. Even now, I still look at the sky and imagine her smiling, even if not at me. Even now, that 0.1% of hope survives—flickering, like a candle about to go out, but still glowing.

What hurts more than heartbreak is spiritual pain—when your soul becomes heavy, not just because someone rejected you, but because the universe seems to have rejected your purity, your honesty, your love. That's not just sad. It's devastating.

So, yes—maybe I was cursed for loving.

But if loving truly, deeply, selflessly is a curse, then I accept it.
I'll carry it with me forever.

Because I'd rather be cursed for loving purely
than be blessed with a love that was fake.

There are wounds that bleed. And then there are wounds that don't bleed at all— but ache every second as if your soul is being torn apart from within. That was the kind of pain I started living with. A pain worse than death. Because death, at least, brings silence. Peace. An end.

But the pain I carried?

It brought screaming silence. Restless nights. Burning mornings. Hollow eyes. And a heart that beat only to remind me that I was still alive when I didn't want to be.

I used to be scared of death once. I'd pray to God to protect my family, to keep my loved ones safe. But after that day—after she looked me in the eye and said *"It's all just timepass"*—I stopped fearing death.

Instead, I started *demanding it.*

Every night I would lie in bed, staring at the ceiling, whispering to the God I once trusted, *"Please, end it. Please just take me. I'm not strong enough. I don't want to wake up tomorrow."*

Imagine a boy, once full of life, now asking for his death—not out of weakness, but because even the thought of living another day without being understood felt like slow torture.

I questioned my existence.
I questioned my birth.
I questioned the purpose of my soul.

"Why me, God? Why did You give me a heart that feels so much? Why did You create a love in me so pure, so innocent—

only to watch it be crushed like it meant nothing?"

It felt like the universe had made a cruel joke out of me. I gave my heart so honestly, never demanded anything in return except to be seen, to be understood—and instead, I was labeled as someone whose love was worthless, embarrassing, and damaging.

That's when I began cursing everything— myself first.

I cursed my heart for being so soft.
I cursed my tears for falling so easily.
I cursed my memories for being so loud.
I cursed my destiny for crossing paths with her.
And I cursed myself... for being born in a world that doesn't value love anymore.

"I'm a burden," I told myself.
"A joke."
"Why did I even come into this world?"

No one noticed what I was going through. No one cared. Not my friends. Not my family. At home, even the smallest mistakes became reasons to scold me. I'd return from school, broken from pretending to smile, only to be shouted at for not keeping my shoes properly or not finishing a task.

They didn't know I was dying inside. They didn't know that behind my silent face was a boy screaming for help, silently begging for someone to ask, *"Are you okay?"*

But no one did.

So I cried alone. Cried into my pillow till it was soaked. Sat in corners of my room with my head between my knees, begging God, *"Why did You do this to me? Why did You make me this way?"*

Some nights I would look at the blades on the table and think... maybe one cut will end the pain. Maybe one moment of courage would silence the storm forever.

But I couldn't do it.

You know why?

Because even in the depths of my pain, one thought would always stop me:

"What if someday… she looks for me and I'm not there?"

Even in that storm of suffering, my love for her saved me from the darkness. That's the irony—*the same love that broke me also kept me alive.*

It's a different kind of curse—to keep breathing not because you want to live, but because you want to stay alive… *just in case* she ever turns back.

Just in case she ever realizes what you felt was real.

Just in case…

I see people getting what they want. I see people being loved, valued, accepted… while I, the one who only asked for *one person*—not fame, not wealth, not even love in return, just a chance—was left begging in silence.

I still remember the way I used to talk to God before she entered my life. I used to close my eyes with faith, bow my head with trust. I used to believe that He had a plan for everyone. That His timing was perfect.

But after she judged my love, rejected my heart, and left me broken, all that faith cracked.

I started praying not with hope, but with anger.
Not with love, but with frustration.
I would sit for hours and whisper:

"Why did You give her to me if You never meant for her to stay?"
"Why did You let me feel so deeply when You knew she wouldn't feel the same?"
"Why did You let me believe?"

Every time I wiped my tears, I'd feel like I was wiping off pieces of my soul. Pieces that I had once built with dreams of us.

I remember the exact moment when I looked up at the sky and said:

"If this is what love feels like, I wish I had never known it."

Because I didn't just lose her...
I lost *me*.

I lost the boy who used to smile for no reason.
I lost the boy who found happiness in the smallest things.
I lost the boy who believed that good things happen to good people.

Now, I walk through my days like a shadow. I laugh when I'm supposed to. I talk when I have to. But deep inside, I am haunted. Haunted by every memory, every plan, every smile I thought we'd share.

And worst of all?
I'm haunted by the version of myself that existed before her.

That boy is gone now. And in his place is someone I don't recognize.

I try to remind myself that maybe, just maybe, God is testing me. Maybe He wants me to be stronger. Maybe He wants me to survive this.

But how long can someone fight a battle they never wanted to fight?

How long can someone carry pain that never ends?

And how do you explain this pain to the world, when no words can hold it?

There is no language for this grief. No vocabulary deep enough for the ache of loving someone so purely—and being told that your love is *timepass*. That it damages *reputation*. That you're better off being *just friends*—when all you ever did was love silently, selflessly, like a prayer whispered every day without expecting anything back.

I feel cursed.

Not cursed because I loved.

But cursed because I loved… in a world that doesn't understand love anymore.

Where feelings are mocked.
Where true hearts are misunderstood.
Where purity is seen as weakness.

I often wonder if I'm being punished for something I never did. Maybe in some past life, I broke someone's heart. Maybe I left someone in pain. And this is the price I'm paying now.

But why does this punishment feel so endless?

Why does this curse feel so personal?

Because even after all this… even after the breakdowns, the sleepless nights, the silent tears, and the rejection—I still love her.

And maybe that's the real curse.

To love someone so much that even your pain becomes proof of your devotion.

Chapter 8: This Is Not Just Love, It Was My Life

After her rejection, I was—no, I am—still broken inside.

People think pain fades with time, but some wounds don't heal. They settle inside you, quietly, like a shadow that never leaves. Since that day, I've been living with a constant ache in my chest. A hollow space where hope used to live. I keep waiting for a light—just one gentle light—that might someday recognize the truth I carry in my heart. Someone who might look at me and see what I felt wasn't obsession or infatuation, but something pure, something sacred. A love so real that even silence couldn't kill it.

But she didn't see it. And maybe she never will.

Still, I made a promise to myself long before her rejection—a quiet pledge spoken not in front of the world but within my soul: *I will not love anyone after her. I will not give my heart to anyone else. If it wasn't her, it will be no one.*

And I meant it. I still mean it.

It isn't because I'm hopeless. It isn't because I can't move on. It's because what I felt for her wasn't just love—it was life itself. It became the air I breathed, the reason I smiled, the prayer I whispered under my breath every single night. She was not just someone I admired; she became the center of everything. And you don't replace the center of your world.

After her, there is no "next."
Only the silence that follows.
Only the promise I swore to keep.

But this love... it changed me. It didn't leave me the same. It forged me—like fire forges steel—into something I had never been before.

Before her, I was just a boy trying to make sense of the world. After her, I became a soul with purpose. A soul that began seeing every woman not just with eyes, but with respect. With depth. With care.

Because of her, I started treating every girl around me with the kind of dignity I always wanted her to receive. My heart, though shattered, became softer—more aware of how delicate people's feelings can be. I stopped seeing girls as just classmates, just people who came and went in life. I started seeing them as daughters, sisters, future mothers, warriors in their own right— people who carried stories, battles, and dreams within them.

I became someone who couldn't stand seeing injustice—not just toward women, but toward anyone. Maybe it was the helplessness I felt when she didn't understand my love. Maybe it was the pain of being unheard. But I knew, from that moment on, I would never let someone else feel unseen if I could help it.

Her rejection didn't kill my love. It redirected it.
It became fuel—for compassion.
For kindness.
For awareness.

And yet, even as I work on myself, even as I try to be better, more aware, more responsible—I'm still beating for her.
Every step I take forward has her name etched somewhere in the background.
Every improvement, every lesson, every moment of strength—it all circles back to her.

She'll never know this, I think.
She'll never know how much I've grown because of the pain she left behind.

Most people think unrequited love is just a phase. That you cry a little, listen to a few sad songs, and then it fades like a bruise. But they don't know the kind of love that shapes your personality. That rewrites your entire belief system. That becomes the very lens through which you start viewing the world.

Her rejection didn't just break my heart. It broke the version of me who once believed life was simple. That if you loved truly, you'd eventually be loved in return. That kind souls always find their reward. But life isn't a fairytale, and some stories aren't written to end in togetherness.

Still, I never cursed her. I never blamed her. I blamed the world—the harshness of our times, the way society reduces love to jokes and lust and trends. I blamed the times we live in, where a heart that feels too much is called weak, and someone who stays loyal is mocked.

But despite all the pain, despite the storm she left behind in my soul, I never let the love die. Because this wasn't a feeling to be switched off. It wasn't a crush. It was devotion. And devotion doesn't fade when it is not returned. It deepens. It scars. It stays.

Sometimes, I sit alone at night and replay everything. The first time I saw her. The first time I smiled because of her. The first time I realized she wasn't just another girl—she was *the* girl. The kind of person who walks into your life not to love you, but to change you forever.

That's what she did.
She changed me.
She *forged* me.

Not into someone who gave up on love, but into someone who learned what love *really* means.

Love, I've learned, is not about dates, or holding hands, or being labeled as "boyfriend and girlfriend." It's not about text messages and Instagram stories. It's about how someone lives inside your heart, even when they've left your life. It's about how you carry someone's name like a prayer, even when you know they'll never pray for you.

This love wasn't a part of my life.
It *was* my life.

I started observing people more closely after her. Not to compare them to her, but to understand how rare what I felt really was. I saw how casually people fall into relationships, how quickly they say "I love you," how easily they move on after breakups—as if feelings were just buttons to be turned on and off.

And it made me realize... maybe my pain wasn't a punishment. Maybe it was proof that my heart had depth.

She might never see that. The world might never value it. But I will. Because in a world that moves too fast, I stayed. I loved. I waited. And even though I'm still hurting, I know that this love made me better.

She made me better.

It's strange how pain teaches you to notice things you once ignored.
Before all this, I used to see the world through wide, carefree eyes. But after her, I started seeing the world differently—deeper, slower, quieter. I began noticing the sadness behind other people's smiles, the hesitation in their voices, the way someone's eyes begged to be understood.

And maybe it's because I knew that pain. I was living it. Still am.

I became more sensitive to others' emotions—not just friends, but strangers too. A girl walking alone in a street made me pause and silently pray she reached home safely. A boy crying silently in class reminded me of myself, and I wanted to tell him, "You're not alone, bro. Even if no one understands, your pain is valid."

That's what loving her did to me. It gave me a heart that aches for others, not just for myself.

Before her, I would've walked away from a fight that didn't involve me. But now? I can't bear to see injustice, even if it's not mine to fix. I stand up. Speak up. And maybe it's not because I'm brave—but because I know how it feels to be unheard.

Her rejection didn't close my heart—it opened it wider.
Wider to the world.
Wider to pain.
Wider to people who feel too much and speak too little.

And through it all, there's still a boy inside me, waiting for someone to notice how deeply he loved.
Not to pity him.
Not to fix him.
But just to acknowledge that what he gave was real.

Sometimes, in my most silent moments, I wonder where she is.
Is she happy?

Does she remember me at all?
Was I ever more than just a name she wanted to forget?

I'll never know. And maybe that's the most brutal truth about one-sided love—you never get closure. You just learn to live without it. You build your life around a space that always stays empty, a name that always makes your chest tighten when someone else says it.

And despite knowing all this—despite knowing she's never coming back—I still love her.

I still wait for a miracle I don't believe in.
I still write about her in my mind when I lie awake at night.
I still look at the sky sometimes and whisper her name, like maybe the wind might carry it to her heart.

But I don't regret it.

Because even if I never get to say it to her again, even if she never knows what she meant to me—at least I know what I felt was pure.

At least I can look in the mirror and say:
"I loved. I didn't fake it. I didn't rush it. I didn't play games. I just... loved."

This is how my love story ends—not with her in my arms, not with a happily ever after, but with silence.
A silence I've learned to live with.
A silence that still carries her name.

She was never mine—not for a single moment.
And yet, I gave her everything.
Every heartbeat.
Every prayer.
Every dream.

I didn't lose her to another boy.
I lost her to a world where feelings are misjudged, where loyalty is doubted, where a boy who loves deeply is laughed at.
She didn't reject me because I wasn't

enough.
She rejected me because she never saw
what I was offering.

And maybe that's the saddest part of all—
being unseen while loving with all your soul.

But if I could go back, if God gave me a
second chance to live this life again...
I'd still choose to love her.
Every time.
Without hesitation.
Without expectation.
Without needing anything in return.

Because that love... made me who I am.

I'm not the same person I was before her.
She broke me. Yes.
But in those broken pieces, I found strength
I never knew I had.
I found a version of myself that was softer,
wiser, more aware of the world.
I became someone who respects every
woman like a sister, who can't ignore
injustice, who notices pain in others' eyes.

I became someone who still loves… even
while healing.

So here's my message.

To every boy or girl who's ever loved
without being loved back—
Don't let their rejection define your worth.

You're not weak because you felt deeply.
You're not a fool because you waited.
You're not pathetic because you cried for
someone who walked away.

You're real.
And real love is rare in this noisy, fake world.

People may not understand you.
They may judge you.
Laugh at your loyalty.
Call you obsessed.
Mock your pain.

Let them.

You don't need the world's validation for
the emotions that come from your soul.
You don't need to be in a relationship to say

your love was true.
You don't need their "yes" to know your
heart was honest.

Some love stories are not meant to be lived.
They're meant to be *felt*.
And that's just as powerful.

So love.
Even if it hurts.
Even if it leaves you shattered.
Even if you have to carry it alone.

Because in loving someone truly, without
games, without masks—you are already
extraordinary.

And to her... if these words ever reach your
heart someday—

Just know:
I never wanted anything from you.
I just wanted you to understand that
someone loved you... in a world where love
is fading.

That someone chose you over everyone else, and never stopped.

That someone still whispers your name—not with anger, not with regret... but with love.

Always with love.

Chapter 9: Why Her Only? Why Not Someone Else?

"Why her?"
"Why not someone else?"
"Why are you wasting your life for someone who doesn't even care?"

These are the questions I've heard more times than I can count. From friends, from people who care, from strangers who barely know me. And every time, I give a small smile, or sometimes I stay silent. Not because I don't have an answer, but because no one is really ready to understand it.

But today, let me answer it—not for them, but for me. For my own peace. For the truth that's been bleeding silently inside my chest for too long.

Why her?
Because when I looked at her, I didn't see just a girl—I saw a story. I saw a feeling I'd

never felt before. I saw a home I hadn't even been searching for, but suddenly knew I belonged to.

It wasn't about her beauty, though she was beautiful in ways words often failed to describe. It wasn't about her perfection — she had flaws, and I saw them. But I loved her not despite those flaws, I loved her because of them. Because she was real. Raw. Honest in her silence. Pure in her detachment. She wasn't someone who chased love or spoke of it easily. She was someone who unknowingly carried it within her presence.

Everyone else felt temporary. With her, I felt *forever*.

And no, I didn't choose her because I had no options. I had people who cared. I had girls who smiled back, girls who spoke kindly, who offered friendship, who maybe would've given me love if I had asked. But I couldn't fake a feeling I never felt. I couldn't lie to someone just because they were ready to give me what she wouldn't. It wouldn't be fair to them. It wouldn't be fair to myself. And it definitely wouldn't be fair to love.

You don't get to choose whom your soul aches for. You don't get to decide who leaves an imprint so deep that no time, no distance, no silence can erase it. That's what she did. That's who she was.

She was the one who made me believe in something more, even when she herself didn't believe in it. She was the reason I started writing again, the reason I learned to feel deeper, to observe more closely, to care with my entire being. And even if she never acknowledged it, she saved me. She gave my emotions a name. She gave my chaos a calm center.

Why her? Because in a world full of noise, she was the only silence I ever wanted to sit with.

Do you know what it feels like to fall in love with someone's essence? Not with their words, or their promises, or what they can give you—but with their presence alone? That's how it was with her. I loved the way she walked past me without noticing. I loved the way her eyes held worlds she never spoke of. I loved the way I could write a thousand poems just from the way she sat in silence.

Maybe people will call me a fool. Maybe they already do. They say I should move on. Find someone who reciprocates. Someone who makes me feel loved. But love, to me, was never a transaction. It was never about receiving.

It was about *being*.

Being loyal. Being true. Being constant even when everything around me was trying to shake me. Being in love even when the world called it madness.

She was not a chapter in my life. She was the ink itself. And that's why it's not as simple as turning the page. It's not about "getting over her" or "finding someone better." Because better isn't a person—it's a feeling. And I haven't felt anything close to what I felt for her.

You ask me, "Why not someone else?"
I ask you—how do you replace a heartbeat?

She wasn't perfect. She didn't always treat me right. She didn't choose me. But even in her silence, even in her distance, she gave me something no one else ever did— *purpose*. Her existence gave mine meaning.

Do you really think I would hold on for this long if it was just infatuation? If it was just a crush? No. I've had crushes. They fade. They vanish with time. But what I felt for her... it stayed. It grew. Even in her absence, it became something larger than me.

And you know what hurts the most? She never even asked to be loved. She never promised anything. Yet I loved her like she was my destiny. Like she was written in my bones before I was born. That's why I never blame her. That's why I never hated her. She didn't destroy me—I loved her knowing the risks, knowing the pain. And I still chose her. Again and again.

So the next time someone asks, "Why her?" I won't explain with logic. I won't try to justify it anymore. I'll just say:

Because sometimes, your heart chooses someone so completely... that no reason, no rejection, no outcome can unchoose them.

And even if she never comes back, even if she never understands what she meant to me—I'll still be grateful.

Grateful that I got to love someone so deeply.
Grateful that my soul got to speak her name.
Grateful that even in the wreckage, I found the truest parts of myself.

It was never about being loved back.
It was about loving right.

And I did. I still do.

Chapter 10: The Final Truth — I Chose Her, Forever

I never told her this.

Not once, not even when I confessed my love for the fifth time. Not even when my eyes were begging her to just understand. I never had the courage to say it.

That I didn't just love her...
I planned to marry her.
To spend my entire life with her.
To protect her from every storm this world could ever bring.

That was always the truth. The final truth I kept buried beneath all my smiles, all my breakdowns, all my silent nights.

Because my love wasn't temporary. It wasn't a passing emotion. It was a decision. A lifetime choice. A vow my soul made before my lips ever spoke a word.

People say, "You're young, it's just a phase." No. This isn't a phase. This isn't a teenage dream.
This was the future I wanted—with her by my side.

I didn't just imagine holding her hand. I imagined standing beside her through every chapter of life—through struggles, through victories, through silence and storms. I imagined coming home from work and seeing her smile and feeling like everything made sense again. I imagined building a life where love wasn't loud, but *constant*. A love that wasn't showy, but *safe*.

She would've never needed to worry about anything. I wouldn't let the world hurt her. I wouldn't let her dreams fade. I would've stood like a wall—silent maybe, but unbreakable. My only dream was to make her feel so protected, so safe, that even the harshest days wouldn't shake her heart.

Yes, I wanted to marry her.
Not to *own* her… but to *honor* her.
Not because I needed her to complete me…
but because she already did.

And even though she never knew, even
though she never saw the home I built with
her in my mind, I still chose her. And I still
choose her—every single day.

People ask, "What if she marries someone
else?"
I'll break inside. I know that. But I'll still
smile from a distance. I'll still wish for her
happiness. Because love, *real love*, doesn't
die when it's rejected—it becomes even
more selfless. Even more pure.

Even if I never get her, she'll still have me.
Whatever I have, whatever I become in
life—she'll always be the one I silently offer
it to.
Whether I become a writer, an IPS officer, a
successful man or just an ordinary one—my
victories will echo her name.

Because every step I take, even now, is driven by a dream that once had her in it.

No, she won't be beside me. Maybe she'll never even know. But my heart will know. My soul will know. And that's enough for me.

They say love is about mutual feelings.
But what about the love that doesn't ask for anything in return?
What about the kind of love that continues giving, even when there's nothing coming back?

That's the kind of love I have for her.

I don't need her to understand. I don't need her to believe in my love. I don't need her to say sorry. I don't even need her to ever come back. All I need… is to be loyal to the vow I made in silence.

A vow that said:

"I will love you in every season of life.
I will protect your name even if you forget

mine.
I will carry this love with me, even if you never carry me in your heart.
And whatever I become, whoever I become—it will be yours."

Because even if the world brings me a thousand options, even if someone else loves me better, treats me kinder—I will never be able to give my heart to anyone the way I gave it to her.

My heart isn't confused. It's not waiting for someone better.
It has already chosen. And it chose her. Forever.

She may never realize what she meant to me. She may never understand how I would've fought the whole world just to make her feel safe. But I did. In my heart, I fought battles every day just to keep this love alive, even when everything felt hopeless.

And now, as I write this, I know the truth more than ever:

I didn't just fall in love with her…
I *committed* my soul to her.
I didn't dream of a relationship. I dreamed of a *life*.
A marriage. A home. A future.

And no matter how much time passes, no matter how much pain I carry—*she* will always be the one I would've married if fate gave me the chance.

Even now, I promise this:

If life ever brings her back to me, I won't need time to think.
I won't need reasons.
I won't ask questions.
I will hold her hand and build the life I once dreamed of—without hesitation.

And if she never comes back?
Then this love will remain sacred. Silent. Eternal.

mine.
I will carry this love with me, even if you never carry me in your heart.
And whatever I become, whoever I become—it will be yours."

Because even if the world brings me a thousand options, even if someone else loves me better, treats me kinder—I will never be able to give my heart to anyone the way I gave it to her.

My heart isn't confused. It's not waiting for someone better.
It has already chosen. And it chose her.
Forever.

She may never realize what she meant to me. She may never understand how I would've fought the whole world just to make her feel safe. But I did. In my heart, I fought battles every day just to keep this love alive, even when everything felt hopeless.

And now, as I write this, I know the truth more than ever:

I didn't just fall in love with her...
I *committed* my soul to her.
I didn't dream of a relationship. I dreamed of a *life*.
A marriage. A home. A future.

And no matter how much time passes, no matter how much pain I carry—*she* will always be the one I would've married if fate gave me the chance.

Even now, I promise this:

If life ever brings her back to me, I won't need time to think.
I won't need reasons.
I won't ask questions.
I will hold her hand and build the life I once dreamed of—without hesitation.

And if she never comes back?
Then this love will remain sacred. Silent. Eternal.

I won't give it to anyone else.
Because this love wasn't meant to be
shared—it was meant to be *kept*.

"*She may never be mine, but everything I
build in this life will still belong to her—
because I didn't choose her for a moment...
I chose her for a lifetime, even if that
lifetime is lived alone.*"

A PRAYER FOR SELFLESS LOVE

Dear God,

I f she's not written for me as a lover,

Then write me somewhere … anywhere…

In her story.

If I must die before she marries,

Make me a pet in her home-

A silent shadow that stays by her feet,

Who wags his tail just to see her smile.

Or … make me a child born from her womb-

So I can be wrapped in her arms,

Call her mother, and still feel her love

In the only way you allow.

I don't care what form-

Just don't keep me away from her
completely.

Let my soul rest where she lives.

Let me exist... where her heartbeats.

Because I didn't just fall in love,

I gave up everything I was... just to stay
close to her.

Final Reflection – From Utkarsh

When I first started writing *Forged in Love*, I didn't do it as a writer. I did it as a broken boy trying to understand what happened to him. I never imagined these words would one day form a book. I just knew that there was a storm inside me—and if I didn't let it out, it would drown me.

This book wasn't written with fancy vocabulary or storytelling tricks. It was written in pain. In tears. In the quiet hours of the night when no one saw me cry. In the mornings when I smiled at school even though I felt dead inside. In the moments when I stared at her from a distance, wishing she could just see… just *understand*.

I wrote this book to breathe again. To give my emotions a home. To say all the things I never got to say to her—and maybe never will.

And in doing so, I learned something I never expected.

I learned that **love is not always about being loved back**.
It's not about happy endings or getting what you want.
Sometimes, love is about becoming who you were meant to be—*because of the person who never stayed*.

She was the spark. The muse. The reason behind every chapter you just read. But more than that, she was the mirror through which I saw the real me. And while she never saw me the way I saw her, I still thank her. Because if she hadn't walked into my life, I wouldn't be who I am today.

I view love differently now.

Not as something that's supposed to be perfect or mutual. But as something *pure*. Something that shows you your truth. My love wasn't returned—but it wasn't wasted.

It became my strength, my transformation, my awakening.

And if you're someone who's reading this while battling your own one-sided love, I want you to know something:

You are not alone.
You are not weak for loving someone who didn't love you back.
You are not a failure for feeling more than they could handle.
You are not foolish for believing in forever—even if they didn't.

If you felt it truly, you're already rare in this world. Don't let their silence , silent *you*.

There's beauty in your heart—even if they never saw it.

So let them go with grace. Let them live their life. But hold on to what they gave you—the pain, yes, but also the lessons, the fire, the strength. Let that love transform you into someone kinder, someone braver, someone who still believes.

She was never mine.
And maybe she was never meant to be.
But she came into my life like a lesson
wrapped in a heartbeat.
And when she left, she left behind a boy
who now knows that his love was his power,
not his shame.

I don't know if she'll ever read these words.

But if she does, I hope she knows—

*I never wanted anything from you. Just
understanding.*
And even if I never got that, I still carry you
with respect... and love.

Always.

— Utkarsh Prakash